Practical Guide on How to Use a Bullet Journal for Better Mental Health

(Anxiety, Mindfulness, Simple Design)

© **Copyright 2018 by Tiana McBoz - All rights reserved.**

This document is geared towards providing exact and reliable information in regards to the topic and issue covered. The publication is sold with the idea that the publisher is not required to render accounting, officially permitted, or otherwise, qualified services. If advice is necessary, legal or professional, a practiced individual in the profession should be ordered.

From a Declaration of Principles which was accepted and approved equally by a Committee of the American Bar Association and a Committee of Publishers and Associations.

In no way is it legal to reproduce, duplicate, or transmit any part of this document in either electronic means or in printed format. Recording of this publication is strictly prohibited and any storage of this document is not allowed unless with written permission from the publisher. All rights reserved.

The information provided herein is stated to be truthful and consistent, in that any liability, in terms of inattention or otherwise, by any usage or abuse of any policies, processes, or directions contained within is the solitary and utter responsibility of the recipient reader. Under no circumstances will any legal responsibility or blame be held against the publisher for any reparation, damages, or monetary loss due to the information herein, either directly or indirectly.

Respective authors own all copyrights not held by the publisher.

The information herein is offered for informational purposes solely, and is universal as so. The presentation of the information is without contract or any type of guarantee assurance.

The trademarks that are used are without any consent, and the publication of the trademark is without permission or backing by the trademark owner. All trademarks and brands within this book are for clarifying purposes only and are the owned by the owners themselves, not affiliated with this document.

ISBN: 978-1-7238-9140-3

Disclaimer

Tips and examples of what you can do to cope with anxiety are further discussed in the book. Before you continue reading, please note that I do not have a degree in medicine. Thus, the suggestions here are based on my personal experience and serve a purpose to share my insights in the hope that it will also help you improve.

If you want to learn more about my journey, you can check out my website: *www.tianamcboz.com.*

TABLE OF CONTENTS

Introduction

Bullet Journal Used for Better Mental Health: What's the Difference from a Traditional Approach?

Core Spreads: Categories

General Part: Description

Bonus Spread

Conclusion

INTRODUCTION

Our brain is run by complex and intertwined processes that can trigger anxiety, panic, and depression. There is no one answer to why this happens, but recent research shows the following as main reasons for the episodes mentioned above:

- Past experiences (childhood)
- Current life position
- Physical and mental health problems

There are many more triggers, but going into all of them will be out of the scope of this book. We will instead focus on how a bullet journal helps mitigate or resolve psychological issues one might experience. For the sake of simplicity, I will call them *anxiety*.

According to the official Bullet Journal website, bullet journaling is *"a customizable and forgiving organizational system."* It combines a planner, to-do list, journal, and sketchbook into one book that is organized in a simple manner. More insights into what a bullet journal is and how to start can be found in my book: "How to Start a Bullet Journal: Inspirational Examples, Creative Ideas, Easy-to-Follow Illustrations."

While some may see bullet journaling as a way to organize their day-to-day life, there are many more advantages to starting this system:

1. *Journaling helps structure your thoughts as you write because this way, you are talking to yourself*

We live in such a fast-paced environment that it is hard to just pause, stop and search for answers. More often than not, there are things we do not want to share with anyone, but they still need to be talked through. **A bullet journal helps identify the underlying causes so that you can act on them.**

This is the idea:

It might help to make a note of what happens when you get anxious or have a panic attack, as this could help you spot patterns in what triggers these experiences for you or notice early signs that they are beginning to happen. You could also make a note of what went well daily, so you become aware that there are positive things in your life too. Eventually, you will start seeing *the glass half full*.

2. *Journaling brings a sense of direction*

Uncertainty has become a big issue in our lives because the world is so dynamic that it is hard to predict outcomes. Stress associated with this dynamism naturally makes people anxious. **With a bullet journal, it is easier to have a glance at what you are aiming to accomplish mid- and long-term because having your plans, goals, and directions outlined in front of you**

helps you act on them. Journaling brings a sense of direction and purpose. You know exactly where you are going because your plans are in front of you.

On par with that, it is also beneficial to be able to track your productivity over time. Since everything is kept inside one notebook, you can clearly see what it is you struggle with and what patterns you have fallen into. This is a great insight, one that you probably might never be able to get if you stick with your haphazard post-it note method.

3. *Journaling eliminates unnecessary worry*

You sometimes ask yourself, *"Can I achieve this?" "Do I have the time to complete this task?" "How can I remember what to do today?"*

It is understandable that to figure whether you can make additional promises or commitments, you need to have a clear overview of your time resources.

Since a bullet journal stores everything in the same place, you will not lose your to-do list (or other 'notes') between days. At the end of each work day, you can make a short list for the following day about what you need to do. That way, you do not have to spend time first thing in the morning trying to remember what you need to do, or trying to remember where you left your list – it's right there in your notebook, exactly where it should be.

Having all your information in one place teaches you to assess if you can squeeze one extra task in between or

better to refrain from it – a crucial time-management skill.

4. Journaling enhances your self-esteem

I know we all hate seeing undone tasks in our planners. If you see that all you have left to do in a day is to email a professor because that box is not filled in, you would hurriedly get it done that day so you can mark the task as complete. It is also rewarding to get to the end of the day or the end of the week and see that everything has been completed. Getting a sense of accomplishment each time is addictive in a good way, so you will make sure to have it repeatedly. Tracking your progress day after day makes you aware of the flaws in your situation, which consequently leads you to take actions. **Overcoming difficulties and documenting it in your bullet journal will make you proud of yourself and raise your self-esteem.**

5. Journaling helps you get to know yourself

Bullet journaling is not just a calendar but a task-tracker, to-do list, journal, place to unleash your creativity, and a place to put down your goals. You can also use it to write down things you are concerned about, whether it is performing tasks at work or making friends.

A bullet journal is a place where you can write down any idea that is on your mind during the day. How many interesting thoughts will you ignore during the day because you claim to be too busy? **If you**

make it a habit to just write things down without necessarily thinking them through, it will help you learn better what you really want to do, your needs, interests, hobbies, aspirations, and a lot more.

Overall, having a bullet journal may be one of the best things that you can do personally; it can motivate you, keep you on track, and help you organize your various events over a specified date. Bullet journaling honestly brings a new point of view to your organization. If you do look into it, recognize that you do not need any fancy paper and pens, just a notebook and pen that provides you with an easy way to organize your life.

Bullet Journal Used for Better Mental Health: What's the Difference from a Traditional Approach?

In this case, the traditional approach is meant as a planner.

The main difference between a bullet journal used traditionally and a bullet journal used for better mental health is your focus.

In practice, this means that:

- *Yearly, monthly, weekly, and daily logs can still be the same:*

You do not have to start your bullet journal in January for it to be effective. Simply begin where you are. If you are reading this in May, your first monthly log will be in May.

- *Your schedules and to-do lists can be altered*:

You will also have some other activities to perform, some habits to work on, some tasks that should ultimately lead to a better mindset. This can include doing yoga regularly, eating healthy, and meditating. We will discuss it in-depth as we progress.

- *The difference is the prevailing content:*

You will have to organize it based on the issues you are facing. Everyone gets anxious for various reasons, so the approach to combat them must also be different. Later in the book, you will see specific topics and examples you can choose from based on your needs. This should help you determine the triggers, develop better habits, become more organized not only in your thoughts, but also in daily life, and get your life back on track.

In the next chapter, you will find suggestions on how to structure the content for your bullet journal.

Core Spreads: Categories

I simplified and grouped the spreads into five major categories:

1. Logging with dates separated
2. Logging with dates combined
3. Graphs
4. Lists
5. Others

I will briefly discuss each of them, outline their benefits, and show you how they look (*general part*). After that, I will give you very precise examples of the topics each of them can contain (*practical part*).

GENERAL PART: DESCRIPTION

1. Logging with Dates (Separated)

This process is fairly simple, and it is more like a monthly spread. In your journal, you can have as many activities and habits you would like to keep track of. Each activity, however, is going to have a calendar for a monthly period. All you have to do is shade the date on which you carried out such activity.

It is called *separated* because you separate activities from one another by always creating a new calendar for each of them. It might be easier to track them later on, but it obviously takes more time to build.

You can use the days of the months (as in picture 1) or the days of the week (as in picture 2).

Take for instance; your goal is to refrain from using social media. On the 5th day of August, you use social media for the first time in the month. That would mean that in your journal, days 1-4 would be shaded while day 5 will be blank. This will show you that you have not been on social media since August began. This way, it will be easy at the end of the month to determine the number of times in a month you engaged in a particular activity or acted in a certain manner.

Below is an image of what it should look like:

Picture 1

Picture 2

2. Logging with Dates (Combined)

This is basically the same as *the separated* with just a very little difference: this gives you the opportunity to combine two (or more) activities that can be grouped under a given terminology. This method of tracking makes the whole process smoother as it is easier to set up and less time-consuming.

For example, with combined logging, if you walked and biked, you can group these two activities as 'exercise' in your journal. That way, it saves you the stress of drawing up another calendar to accommodate the other activity.

In picture 3, you will see the days of the month written horizontally. Vertically, you can use the lines for activities you want to perform.

For instance, on the first line, you will put "walking," on the second line – "biking."

Picture 3

3. Graph

Setting up a graph is a little technical but very achievable. You still have to make use of dates, but this time, each activity has a more detailed outline of how it was achieved daily.

Take for instance; you are trying to track your water intake habit. After having your activity on the first line, you can list out the number of cups just underneath it and also have the day count way below at the end of the page. On day 1, if you drink five cups, all you have to do is place a dot at the intersection. You should do the same for the rest of the month and afterward trace the dots to form a line graph. This way, you get to see your improvements and drawbacks for the specified period. Mind you; this can work for all activities and habits (picture 4, 5).

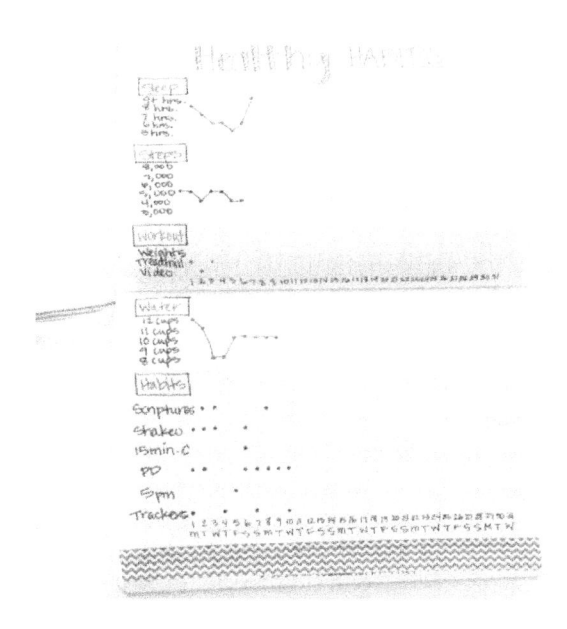

Picture 4

Picture 5

4. List

Another form of tracking involves using the list, and it is very basic and straightforward. It is as the name implies. This method gives you the opportunity to simply list out all your activities and habits.

Take for instance; you are big on exercising. With the listing method, all you have to do is list out the several exercises you did like jogging, biking, push-ups, bench press, etc. under the header 'exercise.' This helps you have a list of all the activities you engaged in.

The same way, you could list activities you want to perform in the future, things you are grateful for, and many more we will discuss later (picture 6).

Picture 6

5. Others

Others are powerful spreads that are not standard, so they fit in neither of the above-stated categories. This can range from writing down several emotions and why we feel them at that particular time to causes of worry. This category covers every other thing that needs to be documented but will fall out of place in other categories.

Now I will make a connection between these spreads and topics you might want to consider for your bullet journal.

Practical Part: Specific Spreads and Topics

Specific spreads and topics will be outlined for each of the main five categories listed above:

1. Logging with dates separated
2. Logging with dates combined
3. Graphs
4. Lists
5. Others

Logging with Dates (Separated and Combined)

For simplicity, I will give topic ideas for separated and combined logging with dates. It is a matter of preference for which one to choose (see above for their differences and description).

Logging with dates is more beneficial to use for the following set of activities as they focus on how many times you managed to perform a particular task. So, in the end, it will provide you with some statistical input on how well you are doing. This one neglects the qualitative part, i.e., your emotions and feelings while you are performing an activity. It solely focuses on how often you carry out such exercise. The exception is the mood/feelings tracker. Derived from the name, they focus on how often you experience a particular feeling.

The overall quantitative nature of such logging is not a deal breaker because, for many activities such as making a bed, it does not make sense to track your emotions and feelings. If you still sense the urge to record your feeling/emotions, you can try to incorporate it as well. This is the beauty of bullet journaling – you can completely tailor it to fit your needs.

So, just start and see how it all goes. If you want to make it more complex by putting additional features, a bullet journal always provides you with the opportunity to do that.

Trackers

Trackers are a critical component for this logging, so I will explain more about them. Bullet journal trackers serve as a guide to teach you more about yourself, raise your awareness of the directions you take and identify flaws in your behavioral patterns. They also help realize what strengths you already have so you can look into how to further improve or maintain the same level.

There are several types of trackers in bullet journaling, but I included only those that I think directly help with anxiety: mood trackers and habit trackers. After that, I will provide specific examples.

a) Mood Tracker

Choose which moods you feel are the most important to track. The most common ones would be:

- Happy
- Sad
- Fear
- Anger
- Disgust

A mood tracker can be a coloring a doodle or square. Some people prefer to select the most prevalent mood of the day and use the color they associate with that mood.

Tracking moods help you have a helicopter view of your emotions throughout a day. To me, it was the first step in the journey to conquer fear, anxiety and a negative outlook on life. Once you are aware of your mood fluctuations, you can take it one step further and ask: Why am I feeling it? What triggered me? Is there a trigger at all, or it is just my habit?

To be honest with you, for me it was often the latter. Habits are formed by our repetition of the same action multiple times. So, if X happens, I am used to feeling Y. In many cases, there is no real need/reason for Y, but it is just my habit. To break through it, create a custom of stopping the performance of a previous habit. For this, use a habit tracker (see below).

b) Habit Tracker

Habit trackers are much broader than the other types of trackers on this list because there is typically a bunch of things you might want to incorporate into your routine by making them a habit of yours.

These trackers serve an informative purpose: to let you know how well you are doing with sticking to a new habit. They are a call to action in some sense, reminding you of the need to put more effort into habit X, or you are doing alright with a habit Y.

Personally, I see habit trackers as a tool to raise my awareness of my existing habits. I think that being aware is always the first step to fight any problem. If we take me as an example,

I typically juggle lots of responsibilities, and it is always hard to switch. Let's imagine I am trying to drink eight glasses of water a day, but I am working on an Excel spreadsheet, and I do not want to lose my concentration. It is easier for me to just cross out one glass in my tracker without getting distracted. In the evening, I can look into this and analyze how well I am doing, but not immediately.

In other words, my preferred way is to simply shade the square (i.e., cross out a glass), carry on with my day and come back to this habit when I have time. Does it make sense?

Now I will give you eight examples of trackers that are easy to implement and explain how to set them up.

Socializing Tracker

You should not shut out the world. Try going out, meeting and talking to new people. As we are social creatures, we are not expected to live in isolation because we need insights from people. Even if you are an introvert, you still need to go out and receive some "food for thoughts" you are going to digest later on your own.

Having connections with the outside world leads to fulfillment. You get to realize that you are not alone in this world. Going out and meeting people goes a long way in helping with anxiety. You successfully created a habit of staying in, so you can do the same with going out and building a relationship. My book "Introvert's Guide on Practical Ways to Start Any Conversation and Improve Your Social Life" could guide you through the process.

How to Set It Up

Heading: Socializing Tracker

Under the heading, place the days of the month (1, 2, 3 to 30) or the week (Mon, Tue, Wed to Sun)

(It does not matter if you go for days of the month or week - just try one approach and change it if you find the other works better).

For every day you make an effort to meet or talk to someone new, shade the day or date on your tracker.

You can leave this journal on your dining table so it is one of the first things you see after you get home and you can fill it right away.

Sleep Tracker

A good night's sleep is incredibly crucial for your health. In fact, it is just as important as eating healthy and exercising.

The other day, I was listening to a very insightful podcast with Matthew Walker here he shared his research and thoughts on sleep. I was so surprised after I found out that sleep deprivation is super dreadful as it can lead to shortening your lifespan and long-term health risks. It makes people more prone to diseases such as Alzheimer's, dementia, and obesity.

The paradox is that we think when we sleep less, we achieve more, but it is not quite true:

> *"Everyone looks like they are busy [at the work place]. It's like stationary bikes. Everyone is looking like they are working hard, but there is no forward progress. The scenery never changes. That's what the underslept workforce will be for you."*
>
> — Matthew Walker

You should listen to the podcast to fully understand the issue, but if you really want to start somewhere right now, I will give you a challenge taken from the podcast: try to get between 7 and 9 hours of sleep every night.

How to Set It Up

Heading: Sleep Tracker

Under the heading, place the days of the month (1, 2, 3 to 30) or the week (Mon, Tue, Wed to Sun)

(It does not matter if you go for days of the month or week, just try one approach and change it if you find the other works better).

Have it close to your bed so you can quantitatively track how many hours you sleep.

Make Bed Tracker

Making your bed is positively associated with overall organization and feelings about starting out a day. If you start your day on a good note, you will set the right mood, which equals you accomplishing more, and being more productive. They say: *"Win the morning, win the day."*

Determination is an essential factor in deciding whether or not to make your bed. You cannot start your day being lazy. So, it is a good habit to incorporate into your morning routine. The way you start your day is the way you live your day.

This little trick can significantly change how you feel about the day and feel throughout your day. It can affect your moods and perceptions of the day in general.

How to Set It Up

Heading: Make Bed Tracker

Under the heading, place the days of the month (1, 2, 3 to 30) or the week (Mon, Tue, Wed to Sun).

For every day you successfully make your bed, shade it on the tracker.

Sports Tracker

There is a link between sports and mental health. It stimulates your brain, activates consciousness and leads to better decisions. While you are running or doing any other exercise, your brain is working actively. This is called diffuse learning, and it is not less important than active learning.

It processes the information that you have taken in during the day. Have you been in such a situation where you had to make an important decision, but you let it go, went to the gym, and slept on it? In the end, you did not think much of it and also did not consider all the advantages and disadvantages to it. However, once you woke up, you knew the right answer. You already made the decision.

I would say if you are suffering from anxiety, see sports as a tool to put you in a better mental health state. It will help you let your thoughts and worries go and make your mind search for solutions.

Just pick one sport that makes you happy, including but not limited to yoga, CrossFit, basketball, cricket, squash – you can choose whatever you want.

For the sake of an example, let's assume you want to start yoga classes. Set a goal: I am going to practice yoga two times a week, 30 minutes a session equals one hour a week.

Did you notice how precise my wording is? So, I know what I am supposed to do.

How to Set It Up

Heading: Sports Tracker/Physical Health Leads to Mental Health/Spiritual Strength

You can be creative with your heading and place something fun in there.

Goal: One hour of yoga a week

Under the heading, place the days of the month (1, 2, 3 to 30) or the week (Mon, Tue, Wed to Sun).

You can have this journal in your gym bag, as it will help you remember to shade the days you meet your target.

Meditation Tracker

There are a lot of benefits associated with meditation. It helps you forget the past or future and be in the present; it boosts mindfulness and consciousness, calms you down, trains your mind not to think of issues, removes worries, and negative energy.

If you are a novice, you can start meditating with some apps. I would recommend "*Headspace,*" but honestly, you can just Google "*Mediation apps*" and choose according to your preference.

Set a goal: I am going to meditate 20 minutes a day for three days a week. So, one hour a week in total.

How to Set It Up

Heading: Meditation Tracker

Goal: 20 minutes a day meditation, three days a week

Under the heading, place the days of the month (1, 2, 3 to 30) or the week (Mon, Tue, Wed to Sun).

Phone-free Tracker

It is scientifically proven that hours without your phone is positively linked with overall happiness.

Newer generations (i.e., Y and Z) are particularly accused of sensing a need for instant gratification. We stare at our screens waiting for *"Hey! What's up?"* as a source of validation that someone is thinking of us. It is a true addiction that can prevent us from doing other things – some of which are as simple as enjoying the world around and being present.

We need to pause and learn that nothing catastrophic will happen if we do not look at our phones for about one hour a day.

Set a challenge: Put your phone aside for one hour before you go to bed.

How to Set It Up

Heading: Phone-free Tracker

Challenge: One hour phone-free before sleep

Under the heading, place the days of the month (1, 2, 3 to 30) or the week (Mon, Tue, Wed to Fri).

During this hour without any distraction, you can focus on yourself, journal, read, meditate or talk to loved ones.

Nightmare tracker

Knowing quantitatively how many times a week you have a nightmare also helps to track the causes. When I analyze such information, I am typically trying to connect the dots and ask myself

- ☐ Did you watch a horror movie before going to bed?

- Did you allow any negative thoughts?
- Did you have a stressful day?
- Are you scared of a particular situation or a bad event occurring again?

Afterward, I move to the second part of my analysis, which I call the "remedy." Here, I am thinking about what could help next time:

- Does it help if you incorporate reading before going to bed instead of watching a movie?
- Does it alleviate your negative thought if you drink lavender tea/meditate?
- Does it help if you avoid talking to your colleague, Paul, during the day?

How to Set It Up

Heading: Nightmare Tracker

Challenge: Figure out the causes/Identify what helps you sleep better

Under the heading, place the days of the month (1, 2, 3 to 30) or the week (Mon, Tue, Wed to Sun).

You can also have this journal by your bedside so you can fill it immediately you wake up.

Morning Routine Tracker

Hit "snooze," do it again, get up, finish your coffee and declaim "as soon as possible; as fast as you can" as your motto in the morning. Get to work, drink one more coffee, and finally realize that your day started two hours ago. Is this you?

As Jordan Peterson states in his book "12 Rules for Life: An Antidote to Chaos," having predictable schedules lead to reduced anxiety.

Every successful person has a morning routine to help start his or her day. Morning routines are powerful such that they set the right mood for a day, give room to think and decide what you want to accomplish, analyze your trajectory and review your goals.

There are lots of recommendations on what a perfect morning routine should look like. Ultimately, it is a trial and error approach, the end result of which you will be able to define what works best for you and come up with your routine.

I suggest starting out with three major activities:

1. Do not look at your phone within the first five minutes of when you wake up. Have a traditional alarm instead of your phone. Put your phone in a different room (i.e., as far as possible if you have just one room) so in the morning you will not be tempted to look at your phone within the first five minutes.

2. Write down three major priorities of the day in your bullet journal. What do you want to accomplish today? Set up a separate section for it (in the Lists format – a section you will discover later on) and place your daily priorities in there.
3. Stretch 10 minutes. Google "stretching" or email me and I will send you my morning stretching exercises + the music I use. Go to my website and fill in the contact form at www.tianamcboz.com, or email me at hello@tianamcboz.com.

How to Set It Up

On one page create one box and make it centric.

Heading: Morning Routine

Under the heading, place the days of the month (1, 2, 3 to 30) or the week (Mon, Tue, Wed to Sun)

Leave some space on the left for lines where you will write your major morning activities. For example:

- On the first line: No phone first five minutes in the morning
- On the second line: Write down three priorities
- On the third line: Stretch

As you can see, it is possible to track almost everything you would like to track. There are tons of examples on the Internet. I gathered those that I think are relevant to the improvement of anxiety.

You can also decide not to use "logging with dates" but a graph or lists for some themes. For example, if you want to track how many times you had a nightmare, use logging with dates. If you focus on the qualitative, i.e., what kind of nightmare you had (describing them) – refer to lists (later section). If you want to measure the intensity of your nightmares, refer to graphs.

For sports, if you concentrate on how many miles you run, you can set it up like this:

Heading: Running

Vertically: miles (1; 1.5; 2, etc.)

Horizontally: the days of the month (1, 2, 3 to 30) or the week (Mon, Tue, Wed to Sun)

So, to know which spread to choose, ask yourself what exactly you want to track.

Graphs

Graphs are good for overseeing trends. In the end, you will be able to judge if you improved your status quo or not.

They are proven to be more visual for people. One quick glance and it is already clear where you are at the moment. This is why a lot of people prefer graphs.

I am not a huge fan of graphs, so I do not use them much. However, I will share why and how I use it.

Sleep Tracker

For benefits of sleep and why it is important to make an effort to track it, please see above.

I tend to run myself to the ground and work more hours than I should. So, when my graph shows a nosedive from eight hours to three, I know I need to act urgently and fix my sleeping routine.

How to Set It Up

Heading: Sleep Tracker

Vertically: 1, 2, 3, 4, 5, 6, 7, 8, 9, 10 (hours of sleep)

Horizontally: the days of the month (1, 2, 3 to 30) or the week (Mon, Tue, Wed to Sun)

When doing your graph, all you have to do is put a dot in front of the number of hours you slept, keeping the dot at the intersection between the day and the number of hours. Do that every day and then draw your line graph to connect the dots.

Your Current State Tracker

For graphs, I do not use a detailed list of emotions/feelings because it looks messy to me (and complicated). I go for three emotions:

Sad

Happy

Neutral

It helps identify a general direction, which is especially helpful when you are just in starting out and having a hard time distinguishing between happiness and excitement for example. There is a fine line between similar feelings, and it can be hard to know where it lies (the feelings tracker is outlined in the Lists section). Alternatively, you can use it if you are busy but still want to track your overall state.

How to Set It Up (see picture 7)

Heading: State Tracker

Vertically: sad, happy, neutral

Vertically (as a continuation): draw the dots

Horizontally or vertically (at the bottom of the page): the days of the month (1, 2, 3 to 30) or the week (Mon, Tue, Wed... Sun)

Picture 7

Time with Your Parents/Friends/Spouse Tracker

If you are a busy person and feel guilty for not spending enough time with your loved ones, this tracker is for you.

I included this one because I was also once too career-centric which left almost nothing for other areas of my life. I put in more than 100 hours a week into working on my goals and felt guilty for not spending enough time with the people I love.

Feeling guilty is detrimental and can develop into psychological illnesses and affect one in many negative ways.

Here's another scenario that may occur:

You are just sitting at home talking to yourself. This is not healthy because keeping your feelings inside creates recurring depression episodes. Ultimately, you will feel isolated and lonely. You will gradually adapt the tunnel view to your problem, as you do not receive any fresh insights into the issue. You could end up believing that no one can understand you, but have you ever tried to take a genuine chance with them?

This graph really helps you see the trend you are following. If the line is always below, you know that you need to act.

How to Set It Up

Heading: Qualitative Time Tracker

Vertically: 1, 2, 3, 4, 5, 6, 7, 8, 9, 10 (hours of quality time you spent with them)

Horizontally: the days of the month (1, 2, 3 to 30) or the week (Mon, Tue, Wed to Sun)

If you want to make it for different people like your spouse, brother, particular friend and so on, you can go ahead and make different spreads.

Lists

Why

It is a spread of reasons as to why a particular behavior, feeling, or emotion occurred. It can work perfectly in combination with the feelings tracker (see below).

Leave a blank spread and list reasons as they come. Analyze them every week and select the ones that occurred most frequently. This way, for the next month, you can already use logging with dates or graph to accurately see the trend of how many times they occurred.

It's important to know the reasons so you can eliminate these events in your life and structure your main reasons. In the end, it will become obvious what reason is the most popular and you can concentrate on working on this.

How to Set It Up

Heading: My WHY

Vertically: numbers 1, 2, 3, 4…

Horizontally: list reasons as they come

Feelings/Emotions Tracker

We have already touched on the importance of tracking how you feel. It raises your consciousness and awareness of different emotions you experienced throughout a day.

It is vital to distinguish between emotions and better understand what exactly you feel.

The real deal, however, is not only about registering the emotions, but understanding the underlying causes and knowing how to deal with them. So, if the feelings tracker is combined with "Why," you get a more advanced technique where you need to ask yourself a range of questions before stating your feelings. For example, if you think you are angry today, ask yourself why.

It might be that you had a client meeting and they told you that the project you have been working on for the past months is not going to happen. You are not overwhelmed by the need to fight or punch them; you are stressed because you do not know what to do next.

Examples of the feelings:

- Irritated
- Sensitive
- Upset
- Anxious
- Tremor
- Stressed
- Angry
- Concentrated
- Distracted
- Happy
- Content
- Aggressive

- Nervous
- Lazy
- Unmotivated
- Sleepy

In the beginning, you may want to cut off similar emotions and leave just one. For example, stressed, angry and nervous. Make it only "stressed" (I am not implying it is the same, I am merely suggesting how to simplify things in the beginning).

It is essential to go through this every week and analyze your behavior by asking why it took place.

How to Set It Up

Heading: Feelings Tracker

Vertically: list the feelings

Horizontally: the days of the month (1, 2, 3 to 30) or the week (Mon, Tue, Wed to Sun)

Favorite Citations

Are there phrases in your life you repeat to yourself in hard times?

I have one:

> "We suffer more in imagination than in reality."
>
> – Seneca

Whenever I am upset, I look at this phrase, repeat it to myself, and somehow it gets easier. I am not sure what kind of magic is behind it, but it works, and that is the most important thing.

As such, when you hear good phrases from successful people, be sure to write them down here. Read through them when you feel down. They will give you hope for when you are going through hard times.

How to Set It Up

Heading: When the Lights Are Off, Look Here

Vertically: numbers 1, 2, 3, 4…

Horizontally: list phrases and citations that suit you

Grateful Journal

Gratefulness is positively linked with an overall perception of happiness. Being thankful, even for small things, helps you see that your glass is half full, not half empty. Our minds naturally register negative things and forget about the positive ones. So, it is easy for us to go down the negative and miserable path while it is hard to stay happy and cheerful.

We need to force our minds to be more positive. One way to do so is to think every day of three things that you are grateful for.

Examples:

- ☐ I am grateful for my spacious apartment.

- ☐ I am grateful for an amazing boyfriend that cares so much about me.
- ☐ I am grateful for a perfect weather today.

How to Set It Up

Heading of the box: I Am Grateful for/Things I Am Grateful for

Vertically: numbers 1, 2, 3, 4…

Horizontally: list them

Basket List/Wishlist

Everyone should have a list of things they want to do/try/accomplish. Put simply, when you have free time, you want to utilize it properly. First, you do not want to spend time searching for what you want to do. Secondly, you do not want to waste your time and make irrational decisions.

For these reasons, it is necessary to have a list of activities you want to perform. It can be as simple as attending a hot yoga class or as complicated as going to Australia.

On a bigger scale, such a list gives you a sense of purpose and perspective. It steers your actions to the direction you took for yourself in advance.

How to Set It Up

Heading: Basket List/Wishlist

Vertically: numbers 1, 2, 3, 4…

Horizontally: list the activities

Picture 8

Compliments

By complimenting yourself every day, you train your mind to see the best in yourself. It boosts your self-esteem.

It is remarkable that if you notice the best in yourself, you see the best in the people around you and the rest of the world. These are the added benefits of such a practice.

How to Set It Up

Heading: Compliments

Vertically: numbers 1, 2, 3, 4…

Horizontally: list them

Self-love

Following the same idea of doing good for yourself, there are ways to show self-love:

- Make a smoothie
- Make a face mask
- Get a massage
- Go shopping for yourself
- Listen to Ludwig van Beethoven
- Sit in a restaurant and grab a bite
- Go to the zoo
- Run for 20 minutes
- Talk to Sarah
- Watch your favorite YouTuber
- Buy that T-shirt you have wanted for a long time
- Meet your friends for a nice chai latte

Try to incorporate this once a day/two days/week etc. to maintain the feeling of happiness.

How to Set It Up

There are two ways you can set it up:

1. As a list where you think in advance of the ways to show self-love. The purpose is to be prepared for the moments when depression kicks in, so you can look at it and implement an activity that will make you happy.

Your setup will look like this:

Heading: Self-care/Self-love

Vertically: numbers 1,2,3,4...

Horizontally: list the activities

2. As logging with dates. In this case, you aim to track how many self-love activities you performed over the course of the month. Doing this will keep you aware if you are doing this sort of activities regularly or tend to neglect them.

How to Set It Up

Heading: Self-case/Self-love

Vertically: number 1 2 3 4 and activities

Horizontally: the days of the month (1, 2, 3 to 30) or the week (Mon, Tue, Wed to Sun)

Picture 9

Affirmations

Affirmations twist your consciousness and make you more positive and certain about life. When you repeat sentences that aim to take you where you want to be to yourself, the odds are higher that you develop a specific mindset/direction where you want to take relevant actions.

There is no miracle to this. If you do not put in any effort, nothing will happen. Affirmations are a perfect tool to help your consciousness recognize successful, fruitful and beneficial patterns you want to follow.

There is only one rule: all affirmations should be in present tense and framed positively.

Examples:

- I know that I am safe.
- I know every emotion goes away after 30 minutes. This negative feeling will pass soon.
- I am beautiful.

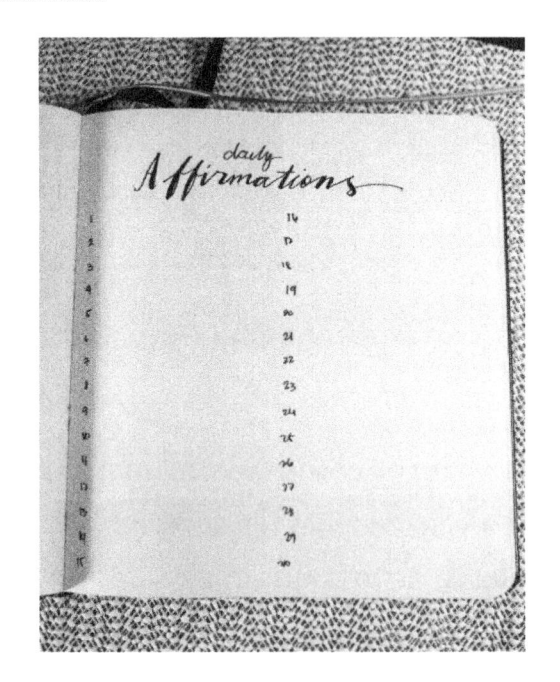

Picture 10

How to Set It Up

Heading: Affirmations

Vertically: numbers 1, 2, 3, 4...

Horizontally: list them

To save space in your journal, you can divide them into two columns (as in picture 10).

Books and Movies

Think about books and movies that you have always wanted to watch/read. They help switch your attention from a problem and move it to somewhere else. However, you need to have a list prepared. Once you do, the only thing you would need is to go and buy/take the book/movie.

How to Set It Up

Heading: Books and Movies Plans/Books and Movies Tracker

Vertically: numbers 1,2,3,4...

Horizontally: list them

You can make two columns: one for books and one for movies.

For me, books, movies, and TV shows are an excuse to enter a conversation, or framed better – to become a part of one. I cannot tell you how many times I have felt left out of conversations with my colleagues when they discuss a movie I have no idea about. I chose to change this by adding a name to my list every time something new comes up.

I use books, movies or shows to get to know a person. I do so by asking simple, but meaningful questions, such as

- "What would you do in his place [in the main character's place]?"
- "What do you think about this scene [someone cheated on their partner]?"

This helps me better understand the values and line of thoughts of the person I am talking to.

My personal list of books to read:

- Rich Dad Poor Dad: What The Rich Teach Their Kids About Money - That The Poor And Middle Class Do Not! By Robert T. Kiyosaki
- The 7 Habits of Highly Effective People by Stephen R. Covey
- Extreme Ownership: How U.S. Navy SEALs Lead and Win by Jocko Willink
- How to Be Yourself: Quiet Your Inner Critic and Rise Above Social Anxiety by Ellen Hendriksen

Other

Dairy

This is a spread for venting your emotions, fears, and flaws. What I learned is that you really have to be open and honest with yourself. This is hard, maybe even harder than opening up to someone. I assume that the reason for this is that if you admit something, you will need to act upon it, and acting is challenging.

The truth is, even if there is no one around you, you will always have yourself. So, you need to try hard to build relationships with yourself, to learn to talk to yourself, identify and deal with issues.

How to Set It Up

Heading: Diary

Blank list: write down everything that is on your mind

I remember when I got burned out; I went on a trip alone and took a notebook with me. I did not want to but continuously forced myself to write down my ideas, thoughts, and emotions. After a few days, I forced myself to re-read them to identify the WHYs.

I found this part to be particularly complex because sometimes what you think in a moment might seem silly so that you are ashamed of it later. But this is a learning curve. Next time, your thoughts will be more coherent and logical.

I also learned to spot the reasons for my behavior, realize flaws in my thinking and understand myself better in general. It did not happen immediately, but with time, it somehow comes to you.

Tip: once you have identified your WHYs, transfer the WHYs to another spread (discussed above).

Core Desired Feelings

Core desired feelings are the feelings you are craving. They could be:

- Comfort
- Happiness
- Adventure

Each emotion has its own source, and you need to get clear on what sources can lead to these feelings. For example:

- Sources of comfort: talk to my mum, go for a walk, read a book, watch YouTubers sharing the same issues, watch a movie;
- Sources of happiness: do nails, dress up in the morning, sign up for Meetup groups (e.g., https://www.meetup.com) and search for a topic of your interest
- Sources of adventure: go on a date with yourself, go on a one-day trip, go cycling, and go for a picnic.

This is done to optimize your time and have the answers ready on what will bring you back to a good headspace.

You can surely log it as a list, but first, look at these suggestions:

How to Set It Up

Spread: make several circles. One circle equals one core desired feeling

You will have three circles in this case. Inside of every circle, write down your 'sources.'

IceBerg

IceBerg is a symbolic representation of your emotional escalation. It helps you to reflect where a feeling started (i.e., what caused it) and observe its transformation (i.e., what stages it went through before it reached the peak). I personally think that it is very visual and helps bring focus and attention to issues.

How to Set It Up

At the top is anger/depression/anxiety - the feeling that you reached.

In the body of the IceBerg, you can list everything that has happened to you over the course of time that you think contributed to this feeling.

The Worry Tree

This provides you with a map of how to get over your negative feelings/anxiety. It helps you understand the underlying reasons for your depression. During down moments, it is hard to think clearly and ask yourself the right questions. So, it is wise to have all the questions prepared in advance and answer them when you face depressing episodes.

How to Set It Up

Heading: The Worry Tree

The first line: Notice the worrier

The second line: What am I worried about?

See picture 11 for inspiration, but feel free to work out your own set of questions.

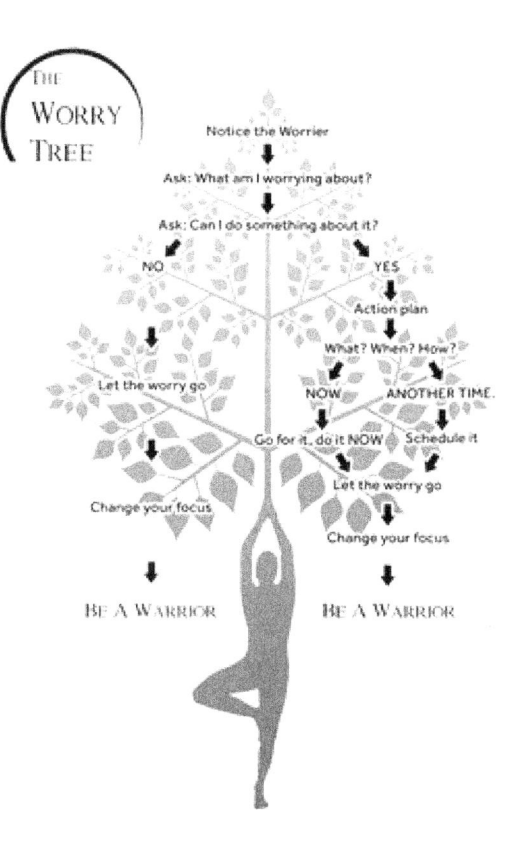

Picture 11

Bonus Spread

How to Keep a Bullet Journal

A spread about keeping a bullet journal probably sounds weird and fascinating. Plan around and track if you managed to use your bullet journal as you should have. Doing this will help you keep tabs on how well you are journaling. You are just embarking on developing this new habit, so do not expect too much from yourself. Move at a steady pace and achieve progress slowly. It is totally OK to fail to do it today as long as you carry on tomorrow.

The important thing you should remember here is that the bullet journal is your helper, not your boss. You are the boss; you manage your bullet journal. The primary purpose of adopting a bullet journal in the first place is to improve. So, keep this in mind along your journey.

How to Set It Up

Make it as logging with dates.

Heading: Bullet Journal Routine

On the page draw 30 (or the number of days the month actually has) squares or circles. One line in one week equals seven squares. So, you will have approximately five lines.

Cross out one square every time you manage to spend time on your bullet journal.

At the end of each week, state the number representing how many times you failed to manage it. Write it at the end of the line.

For example,

Square   square   square   ~~square~~   square   square   ~~square~~   2

So, in this example 2 means that a person has failed to keep their bullet journal on Thursday and Sunday.

Conclusion

Most people experience constant stress for many reasons: we rush to work, we have bills to pay, we have debts, we have kids to take care of, and then we have personal issues with our loved ones.

All of these are recipes for anxiety to develop. Unfortunately, more often than we wish, they stay under the radar because the person does not recognize the symptoms or does not want to tackle it in such a fast-paced world.

Usually, when someone mentions anxiety, we think of something detrimental. However, it does not necessarily mean that people are constantly experiencing anxiety. It could be just one episode a week, or some particular situations in life that cause a state of worry, anxiousness, nervousness, and fear. These emotions are triggered by the body's natural stress response to let us know that something is wrong.

The tools explained in this book will go a long way in helping you manage your anxiety; they are very easy to understand and implement. With them, you will know the activities or habits that trigger different emotions, and with that information, you can figure out how to tackle them.

Although the suggested spreads are very simple, you can always make it more complex as you progress. Do not worry at all about making it perfect. The principal goal is that it should work for you. Do not over think it, just start.

You can read many books and take all the knowledge in, but the moment it starts working for you is the moment when you really want it to work.

Do you still have any questions? Go to my website for relevant content: www.tianamcboz.com, or send an email at hello@tianamcboz.com.

Printed in Great Britain
by Amazon